10/29/14

W9-DFN-332

JNF

Withdrawn

Be a
Community
Leader

How to Write
an Op-Ed Piece

Leslie Harper

PowerKiDS press
New York

Published in 2015 by The Rosen Publishing Group, Inc.
29 East 21st Street, New York, NY 10010

First Edition

Editor: Norman D. Graubart
Book Design: Joe Carney
Book Layout: Colleen Bialecki
Photo Research: Katie Stryker

Library of Congress Cataloging-in-Publication Data

Harper, Leslie.
How to write an op-ed piece / by Leslie Harper. — First edition.
    pages cm. — (Be a community leader)
Includes index.
ISBN 978-1-4777-6685-9 (library binding) — ISBN 978-1-4777-6686-6 (pbk.) —
ISBN 978-1-4777-6687-3 (6-pack)
1. Editorials—Authorship—Juvenile literature. I. Title.
PN4784.E28H37 2015
808.06'607—dc23
                              2014001397

Manufactured in the United States of America

CPSIA Compliance Information: Batch #WS14PK3: For Further Information contact Rosen Publishing, New York, New York at 1-800-237-9932

Contents

Sharing Your Opinion

Do you ever read newspapers or news magazines? Do you enjoy reading news websites on the Internet? Reading newspapers and other sources of news is a great way to stay informed about the world.

When you read a news story about an event, you may notice that it is filled with facts. These facts will include where the event happened, who was there, and what happened. When newspaper and magazine reporters write news stories, they generally stick to facts and avoid writing **opinions**. However, there is one section of the newspaper where people are encouraged to share their opinions. On the op-ed page, people who do

You may want to ask your parents for a subscription to a newspaper if they don't already have one.

4

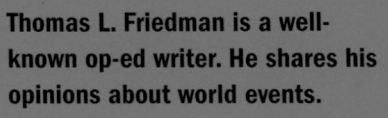

not work for the newspaper can write essays that express an opinion on an issue.

People who have special knowledge about a topic or are very passionate about a certain issue often write op-ed pieces. While many are written by adults, anyone is free to write and submit an op-ed piece. Writing an op-ed piece gives kids and adults a chance to share their opinions on issues that matter to them!

Op-Ed Tip

Facts are pieces of information that can be proven true. Opinions are beliefs based on what a person thinks. Saying pizza is a type of food is a fact. Saying pizza tastes better than broccoli is an opinion. Sometimes facts and opinions can be tricky to tell apart. Can you think of other examples of facts and opinions?

5

Choosing a Topic

Op-ed pieces are a type of **persuasive** writing. That means their purpose is to persuade, or convince, readers to change their minds to agree with the writer's opinion. By writing a strong and effective op-ed piece, you may change someone's mind about an important issue in your town. Is there anything in your neighborhood or city that you would like to see change?

This woman is trying to persuade her coworkers to follow her idea for their business. Persuasion is an important life skill.

If you want to convince your town to add bike lanes, an opinion piece is a great way to raise awareness about your cause.

The first step to writing an op-ed piece is choosing a topic, or issue, to write about. You can begin by thinking about what is important to you. Do you like to read or use computers? If so, you might think that your local library should get more money to spend on new books and computers. If you enjoy being outside, you might think an empty lot in your neighborhood would be a great place to build a new park. Perhaps you ride a bike to school and think bike riders would be safer if your city or town put bike lanes on the roads.

When writing an op-ed piece, it is very important to stick to one issue and one opinion. Most op-ed pieces are not very long. Because you have a limited amount of space to share your opinion, you should keep your ideas simple and clear. Tell readers about one problem and then give them one possible solution.

Let's say, for example, that you plan to write your op-ed piece about bike lanes. You might believe that riding a bicycle to school is a great way to get exercise. You may also think that riding a bike to school is tiring and that the school cafeteria should serve a healthier breakfast in the morning.

> Your word processor should have a feature called Word Count. This will tell you how many words are in your piece.

Word Count

● ● ●

Current selection
Words: 179
Characters: 955

Whole document
Words: 369
Characters: 2018

OK   Help

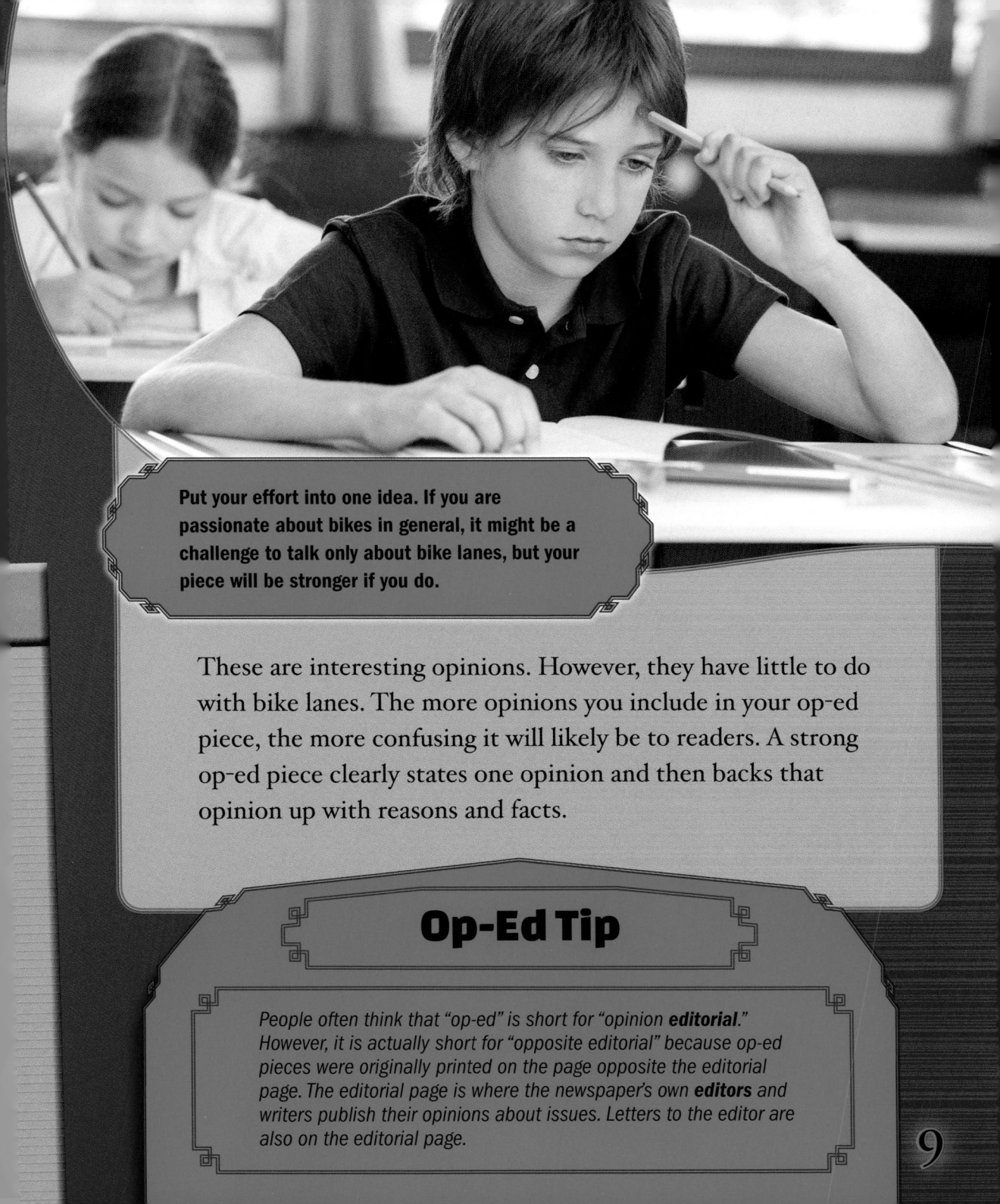

Put your effort into one idea. If you are passionate about bikes in general, it might be a challenge to talk only about bike lanes, but your piece will be stronger if you do.

These are interesting opinions. However, they have little to do with bike lanes. The more opinions you include in your op-ed piece, the more confusing it will likely be to readers. A strong op-ed piece clearly states one opinion and then backs that opinion up with reasons and facts.

Op-Ed Tip

People often think that "op-ed" is short for "opinion **editorial**." However, it is actually short for "opposite editorial" because op-ed pieces were originally printed on the page opposite the editorial page. The editorial page is where the newspaper's own **editors** and writers publish their opinions about issues. Letters to the editor are also on the editorial page.

Pick a Paper

Some newspapers are given out for free, while others are sold. Some are written for a certain **audience**, or group of readers, while others are written for a general audience. School newspapers, for example, are usually written by and handed out to students of one particular school. The articles in these papers may include news about events around town or important current events. However, most of the information will relate to the school. The audience is primarily students, though some teachers and parents may read the paper, too.

This newsstand carries all kinds of newspapers. Some have local news, while others have national or international news. Others may focus on business.

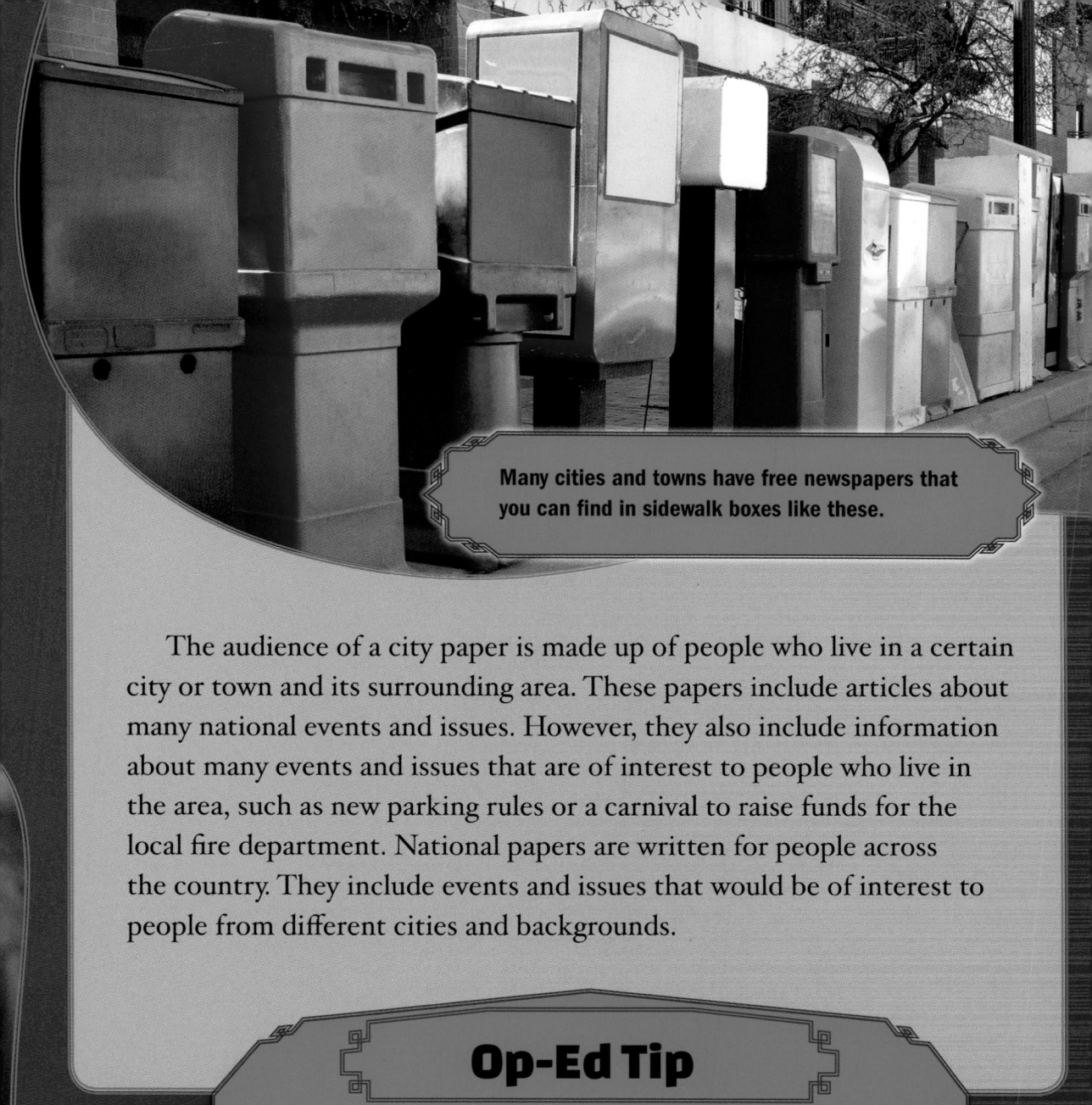

Many cities and towns have free newspapers that you can find in sidewalk boxes like these.

The audience of a city paper is made up of people who live in a certain city or town and its surrounding area. These papers include articles about many national events and issues. However, they also include information about many events and issues that are of interest to people who live in the area, such as new parking rules or a carnival to raise funds for the local fire department. National papers are written for people across the country. They include events and issues that would be of interest to people from different cities and backgrounds.

Op-Ed Tip

Newspapers that are published every day are called dailies. Those published every week are called weeklies. It is important to find out how often your periodical is published. If your city will be voting on bike lanes next week, make sure the paper you choose will publish your piece before then.

Deciding which paper to submit your op-ed piece to will depend on the issue and the audience you would like to reach. If your issue is directly related to your school, you might choose your school paper. If your town's local government will decide the issue, a city paper may be a better choice. Bike lanes are probably of interest to many kids in your school. However, it is the adults in your town who will likely be voting on the issue.

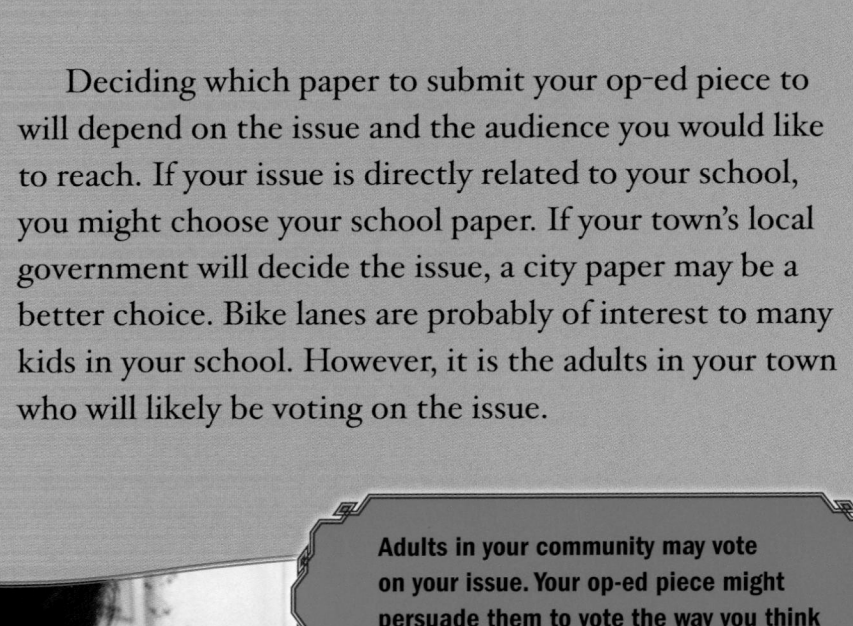

Adults in your community may vote on your issue. Your op-ed piece might persuade them to vote the way you think they should.

Editors are skilled readers and writers. If you are excited about your piece when you talk to an editor, he will want to help you succeed.

Once you have chosen a newspaper, you can look in a copy of the paper or on the Internet for information on how to submit an op-ed piece. If you can, find out how to contact the editor who works on the paper's op-ed page. An editor is a person who checks facts, corrects mistakes, and decides what will be printed in the newspaper. This person or someone from his or her office should be able to tell you how long your op-ed piece should be and the best way to submit it to the paper if you can't find this information on the website.

Exploring Op-Ed Examples

Reading examples of op-ed pieces is a great way to understand the style used and the way opinions are presented. Start by reading op-ed pieces from the paper to which you will submit your piece. This will give you a good idea of the general length and language used. You can also see if the newspaper has published any other recent op-ed pieces related to your topic.

Get an idea of the word count for an op-ed piece. Generally, op-eds are short. Keeping the piece short helps the reader understand the issue and the opinion quickly.

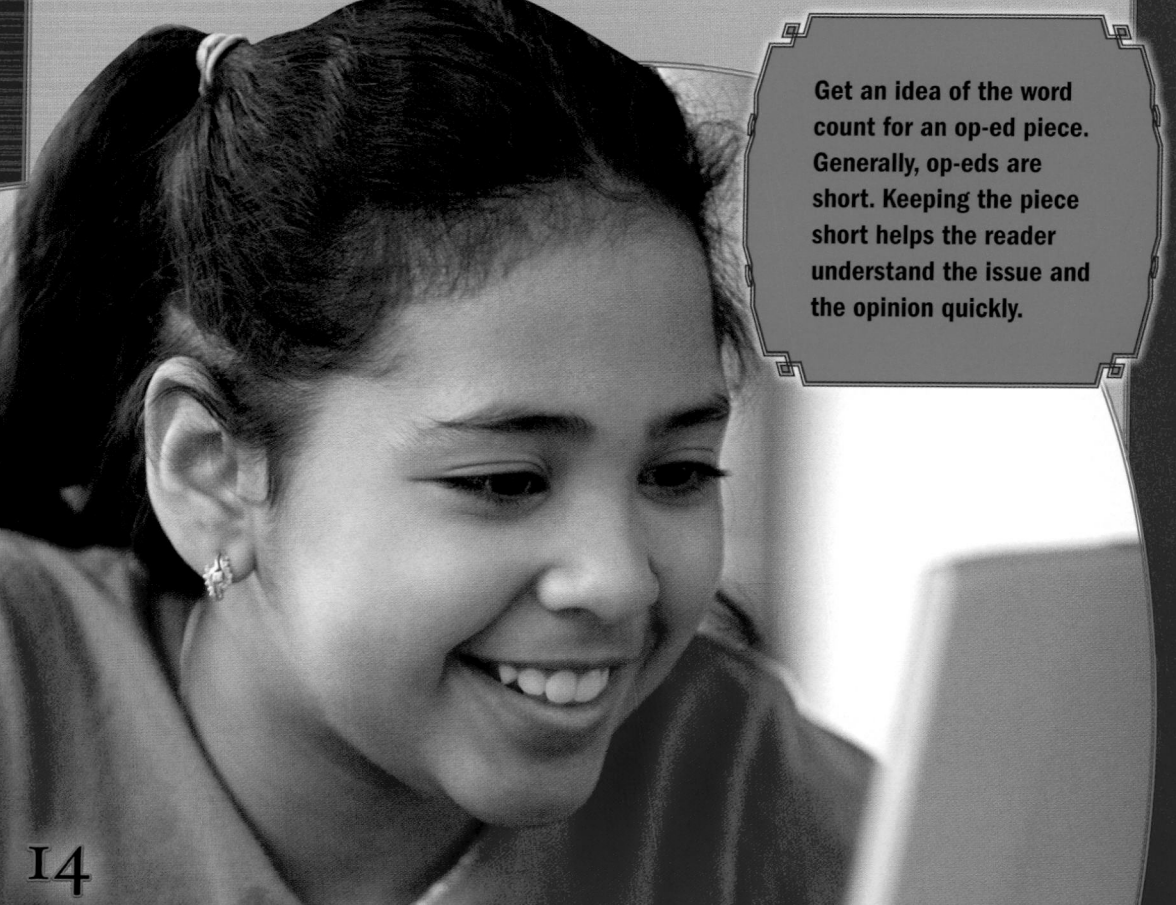

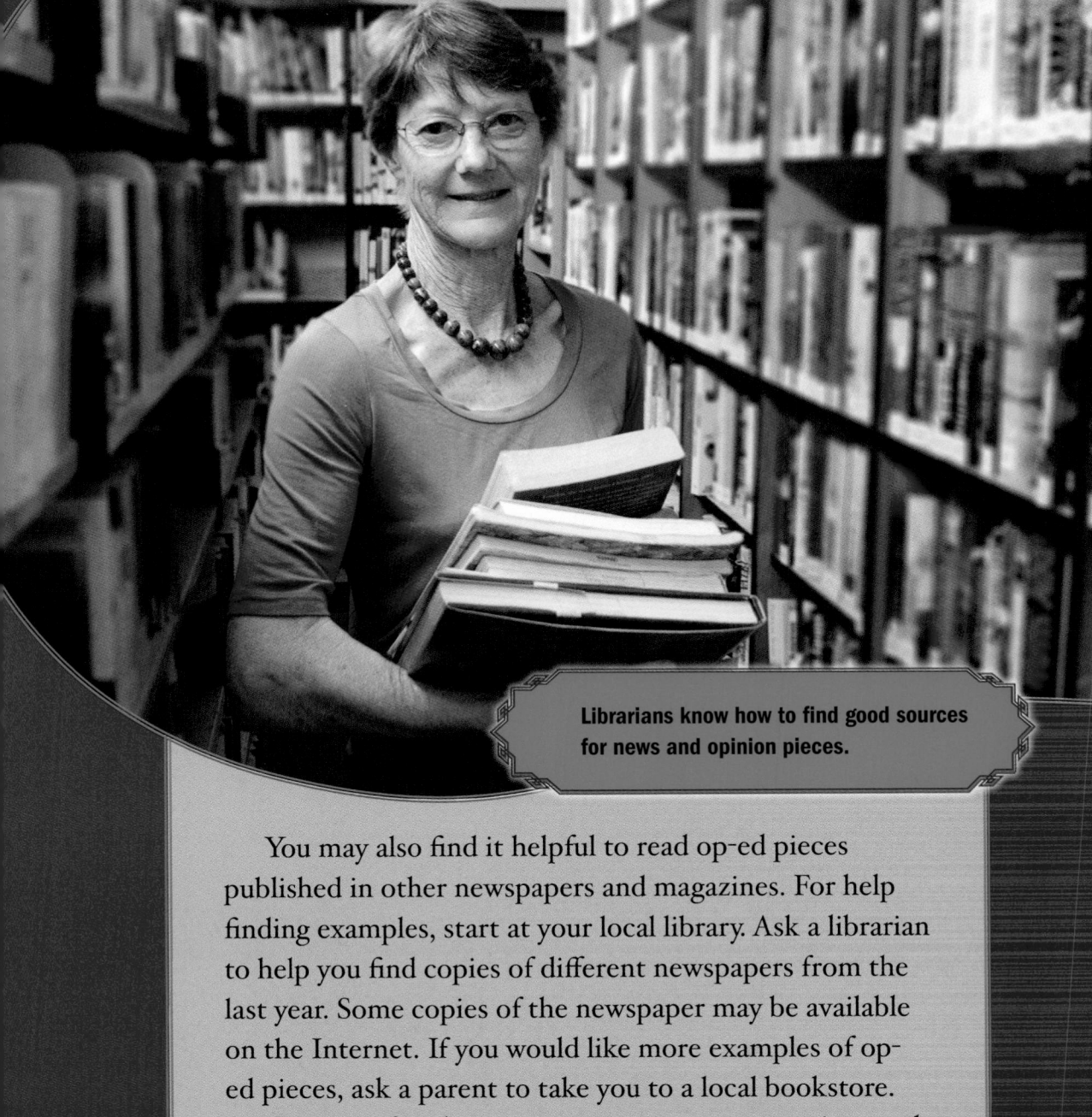

Librarians know how to find good sources for news and opinion pieces.

You may also find it helpful to read op-ed pieces published in other newspapers and magazines. For help finding examples, start at your local library. Ask a librarian to help you find copies of different newspapers from the last year. Some copies of the newspaper may be available on the Internet. If you would like more examples of op-ed pieces, ask a parent to take you to a local bookstore. Bookstores often have many current news magazines and copies of several city and national newspapers that you can look through.

Ready for Research

An effective op-ed piece will include **evidence**, or facts that back up the writer's opinion. To find these facts, you will need to **research**, or carefully study, your issue to find out more about it. For your op-ed about bike lanes, you may want to find out how many people in your town ride bicycles regularly and how many kids ride bikes to school. You may also want to find information about traffic accidents in your town involving bicycles. To show readers how bike lanes could fix the problem, look at **data** from other cities that already have bike lanes. Have the bike lanes in those places made biking safer?

Look for writing contests online or at school. Practicing your writing is very important.

SUBMISSION

Your school is a great place to begin your research. Talk to your teachers and your school librarian or media specialist. They can suggest helpful books, encyclopedias, newspapers, and websites for finding information on your topic. If you do use the Internet, be sure the websites you use are **credible**, or truthful. Websites run by museums, zoos, and government agencies are good places to start.

Op-Ed Tip

Be sure the sources you use are current, or up-to-date. If you are not careful, you might include old data about your subject. This may make people less trusting of your writing. To be sure your information is correct, try to find at least two sources that agree on each fact you include.

Jump into Writing!

Once you have gathered information from your research, it is time to begin writing. A first attempt at writing something is called the **first draft**. When it is finished, you can go back and make changes. Do not be afraid to get started!

Your op-ed will be most effective with a strong **structure**, or form, that will keep your ideas organized and clear.

A first draft is not your final product. Professional writers sometimes write several drafts.

FLOWCHART OF AN OPINION PIECE

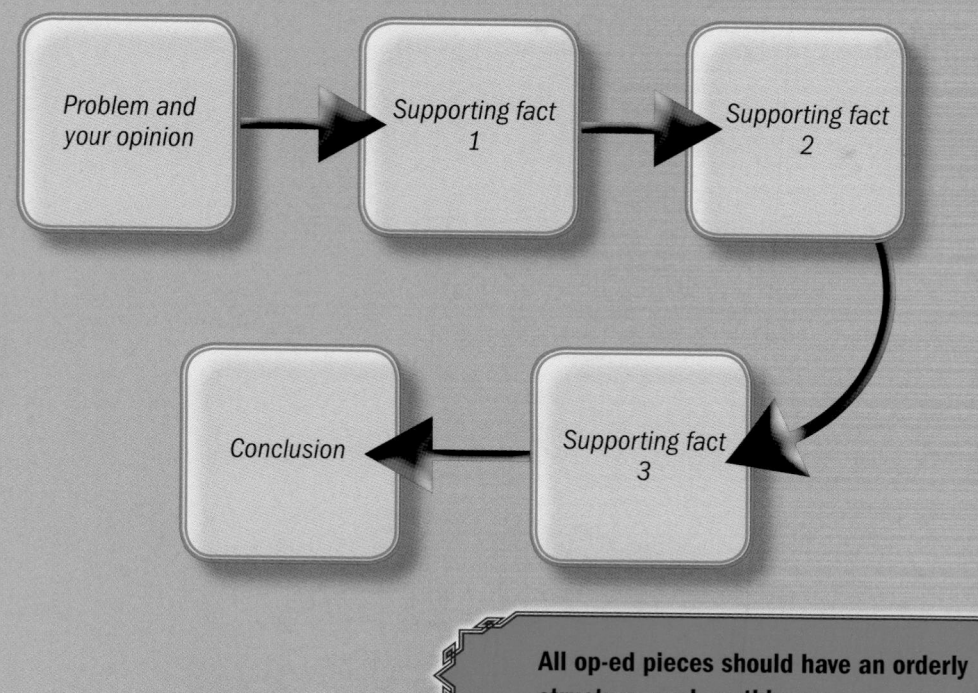

Problem and your opinion → Supporting fact 1 → Supporting fact 2 → Supporting fact 3 → Conclusion

All op-ed pieces should have an orderly structure, such as this one.

Begin with an introduction, which presents the issue to your readers. This is where you will state the problem and your opinion on the best way to fix it. The next section of your piece will give supporting facts that show why you believe your opinion is correct. For example, this is where you might say that a study from a university in Canada showed that bicyclists are 10 times more likely to be injured riding on a busy street than in a separate bike lane. Your piece will end with a conclusion, which will summarize, or restate, your opinion.

Your research will be very helpful to you while you write. Having credible and current facts and data allows you to be very specific when you state your evidence. For example, you can say a study in the city of Phoenix, Arizona, found that 95 percent of bicycle accidents in the city happened on streets with no bike lanes. Be sure to **cite** your sources of information. This lets people know that the information came from trusted sources. They can also find out more for themselves if they would like.

Research can take a long time. It's important to use good sources, though. Don't rush your work by using incorrect information.

When you have finished your first draft, read it over a few times. If you feel like it needs more evidence, go back to your sources and do some more research. You may find it very helpful to go back and compare your draft to the examples you read of other op-ed pieces. Does the structure of your piece look similar to the other examples? Do the tone and language sound similar?

Op-Ed Tip

When writing for a newspaper, you should keep your language formal. Formal language adds strength to your writing. Even if you are writing for a school newspaper, formal writing is better than informal writing. If you take the time to polish your language, readers might even forget that a kid wrote the article!

21

Read and Revise

Now that the first draft of your op-ed piece is finished, you have the chance to make it even better! This is done through editing and **revising**. Editing is checking for and correcting any mistakes in spelling and grammar. Most word-processing programs will check your spelling for you. However, it is still important to read your piece through and keep an eye out for any mistakes you may have missed. You should also read the piece through to check for any mistakes in grammar. Grammar is the system of rules for how words combine to form sentences.

English Usage

THESAURUS

A thesaurus lists words with similar meanings. These reference books can help you avoid repetition in your writing.

Many types of writing use only one tense throughout. However, your op-ed piece may use several. For example, you might write that more than 100 accidents between cars and bicycles occurred in your town last year. Today, many kids are afraid to ride their bikes on busy streets. If bike lanes are created, they will make kids safer. These sentences are examples of past, present, and future tense. As you read your piece, make sure you have used each tense correctly.

Make sure that your ideas progress in order. You don't want to confuse the reader.

One thing to keep in mind when you are making changes is word count, or how long your piece should be. When you have corrected any mistakes and your piece is the right length, try reading it out loud. Reading it to yourself will let you hear how the piece flows from one idea to the next. If you read it aloud to others, such as friends and family, they can also give you notes, edits, suggestions, and other **feedback**. You can also ask a parent, teacher, or librarian to read the piece for you and offer feedback. These adults are part of your audience. If something does not make sense to them, many others will likely feel the same way.

You can read your op-ed out loud to a parent. This may help you find any remaining problems with your piece.

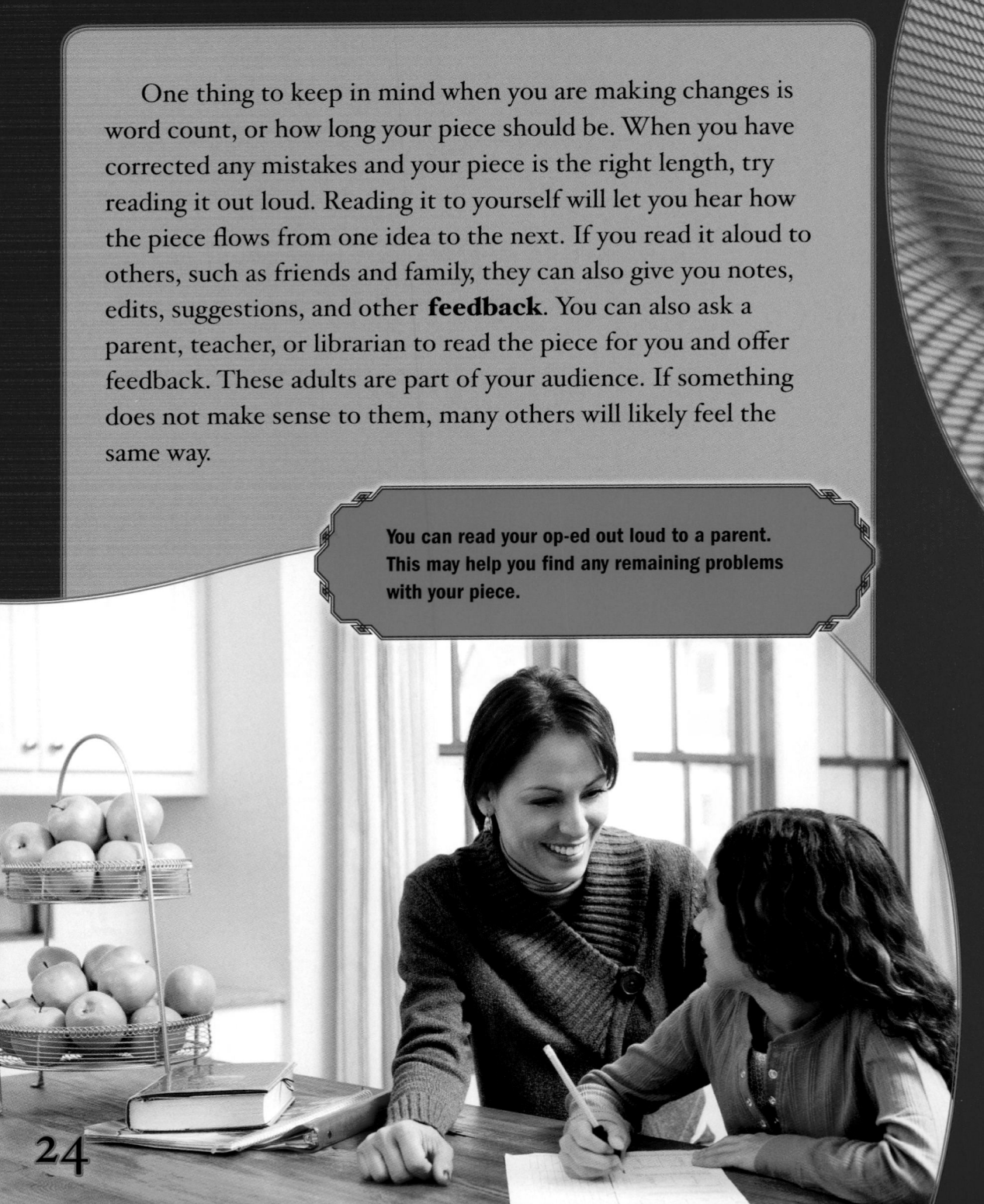

Save early drafts of your op-ed! You may want to keep a phrase or idea that you had edited out earlier.

Revising a piece of writing means reading it again and making changes. As others read your piece and offer suggestions, do not be afraid to move large chunks of text around or rewrite entire sections. Your op-ed piece is finished only when you are happy with it!

Getting Published

When you have a finished op-ed piece, it is time to send it to the newspaper you have chosen. Many newspapers will give you the option of sending in your piece through either fax or email. Some have online forms for submission. If you are sending your piece through email, be sure the document is in the correct format and that it is named correctly. Some newspapers do not accept emails with attachments, so be sure to follow their directions. If you are unsure about any of the requirements for submission, contact the newspaper again and get the answers you need.

When you send off your piece, keep in mind that it may not be published in the newspaper. Newspapers, even small ones, get many op-ed pieces sent in on many different topics. There may be any number of reasons why they do not choose to print yours. However, you should not feel bad! You can try sending your piece to another paper or even publishing it yourself on a blog. You could also pass it out as a flyer in your neighborhood!

This is the New York Times Building. Newspapers the size of the *New York Times* usually want you to send your op-ed in by email.

Op-Ed Tip

If you need to send your piece through email, ask your parents for help. If you do not have your own email account, they may send it through one of their accounts for you.

27

New Media

Publishing your op-ed piece in a newspaper is a great way to reach many readers at once. However, it is not the only way to share your opinion. More and more people get their news and information from the Internet. Some websites are related to newspapers, magazines, and television news programs. Many others are run by people or groups who support a cause.

You can read a lot of newspapers on iPads and other tablets.

26 JUNE

BIKE LANES

TAGS: INTERNET, BLOG

Many cities all over the United States are adding bike lanes to their roads. This is a big step toward making our cities safer. Bike lanes allow bike riders and cars to use their own lanes while riding and driving...

 128   32

e Share   Tooot

http://www.leremy.com/webdesign/100234533563242   PERMALINK

COMMENTS (58)

KEEPING STREETS SAFE

TAGS: INTERNET, BLOG

08:32 ———————————— 12:15

CATEGORIES

‖ Bikes

‖ Local Issues

This is an example of a blog. There are many websites that can host your blog for free.

Publishing your op-ed piece on the Internet means people all around the world might see it!

If you would like to share your op-ed piece on the Internet, do some research first. Find a website related to either your city or your issue. For example, you might send your piece on bike lanes to a community website or a website about bicycling. You may even decide to start your own blog or website! When you publish anything on the Internet, be very careful not to share any personal information with anyone you do not know.

Keep Writing!

Writing clearly and effectively is a very important skill. If you enjoyed writing your op-ed piece, go ahead and write another one! You may have several interesting ideas about how to make your school, neighborhood, city, and country better places.

If you would like to keep working on the first op-ed piece you wrote, consider revising some more. You might want to make the piece longer and send it into a magazine. You could even turn your piece into a letter and send it to a member of your local government, such as a mayor or state senator. As with any skill, the more you practice writing effectively, the better you will become!

> Writing well is an important life skill. If you can convince people with your words, you might become a professional writer someday!

Glossary

audience (AH-dee-ints) A group of people who watch, listen to, or read something.

cite (SYT) To call attention to or give credit to a source.

credible (KREH-duh-bel) Believable and trustworthy.

data (DAY-tuh) Facts in the form of numbers.

editorial (eh-duh-TAWR-ee-ul) An article in a newspaper or magazine that gives the opinion of the top editors or publisher.

editors (EH-duh-terz) People who correct mistakes, check facts, and decide what will be printed in a newspaper, book, or magazine.

evidence (EH-vuh-dunts) Facts that prove something.

feedback (FEED-bak) Suggestions from people who have reviewed something.

first draft (FURST DRAFT) The first attempt at writing a piece.

opinions (uh-PIN-yunz) Beliefs that are based on what people think rather than what is known to be true.

persuasive (per-SWAY-siv) Able to make someone agree.

research (REE-serch) To study something carefully to find out more about it.

revising (rih-VYZ-ing) Making changes to or improvements in something.

structure (STRUK-cher) Form.

Index

Websites

Due to the changing nature of Internet links, PowerKids Press has developed an online list of websites related to the subject of this book. This site is updated regularly. Please use this link to access the list:
www.powerkidslinks.com/beacl/oped/